SandCastle™

Perfect Pets

Cuddly Cats

Anders Hanson
AUTHOR

C.A. Nobens
ILLUSTRATOR

Consulting Editor, Diane Craig, M.A./Reading Specialist

ABDO
Publishing Company

Published by ABDO Publishing Company, 4940 Viking Drive, Edina, Minnesota 55435.

Printed in the United States.

CREDITS

Edited by: Pam Price

Concept Development: Nancy Tuminelly

Cover and Interior Design and Production: Mighty Media

Photo Credits: Comstock, JupiterImages Corporation, Cavignaux Régis/BIOS/Peter Arnold, Inc.,
Labat Jean-Michel/PHONE/Peter Arnold, Inc., Photodisc, ShutterStock

LIBRARY OF CONGRESS CATALOGING-IN-PUBLICATION DATA

Hanson, Anders, 1980-
  Cuddly cats / Anders Hanson ; illustrated by C.A. Nobens.
     p. cm. -- (Perfect pets)
  ISBN-13: 978-1-59928-745-4
  ISBN-10: 1-59928-745-5
  1. Cats--Juvenile literature. I. Nobens, C. A., ill. II. Title.

  SF445.7.H37 2007
  636.8'083--dc22

                              2006034400

SandCastle™ books are created by a professional team of educators, reading specialists, and content developers around five essential components—phonemic awareness, phonics, vocabulary, text comprehension, and fluency—to assist young readers as they develop reading skills and strategies and increase their general knowledge. All books are written, reviewed, and leveled for guided reading, early reading intervention, and Accelerated Reader® programs for use in shared, guided, and independent reading and writing activities to support a balanced approach to literacy instruction.

SandCastle Level: Transitional

LET US KNOW

SandCastle would like to hear your stories about reading this book. What is your favorite page? Was there something hard that you needed help with? Share the ups and downs of learning to read. We want to hear from you! To get posted on the ABDO Publishing Company Web site, send us e-mail at:

sandcastle@abdopublishing.com

CATS

Cats are cute, playful, affectionate pets. They can be very active, but they also like to curl up in your lap for a cuddle.

Angelina chooses a kitten at an animal shelter. Animal shelters have many cats waiting for good homes.

Miguel feeds his cat every day. He also makes sure his cat has fresh water.

Jayden plays with his kitten. It is fun, plus it is good exercise for his kitten.

Riley scoops out her kitten's litter box every day. She changes the litter once a week.

Leah takes her cat to the veterinarian for a checkup. The vet makes sure Leah's cat is healthy.

A Cat Story

Colin has a cuddly cat that is a curious calico. Coco follows Colin wherever he may go.

When Colin brushes his teeth in the morning, Coco jumps in the sink without a warning!

For homework tonight,
Colin studies a map.
Suddenly Coco
leaps into his lap.

And when Colin
snuggles into bed,
that cuddly Coco
sleeps by Colin's head.

Fun facts

A cat can be right-pawed or left-pawed.

Cats have 32 muscles in each ear.

There are about 100 breeds of cats.

A cat can sprint at about 31 miles per hour.

A cat will spend nearly one-third of its life grooming itself.

The first cat show was held in 1871 at the Crystal Palace in London.

Glossary

affectionate – being loving and tender.

calico – a tri-color cat with patches of white, black, and orange.

cuddle – to hug or hold close.

scoop – to remove or gather using a small shovel.

shelter – a place where people or animals who are hurt or need a home can stay.

snuggle – to curl up with or draw close for comfort and affection.

veterinarian – a doctor who takes care of animals.

About SandCastle™

A professional team of educators, reading specialists, and content developers created the SandCastle™ series to support young readers as they develop reading skills and strategies and increase their general knowledge. The SandCastle™ series has four levels that correspond to early literacy development in young children. The levels are provided to help teachers and parents select appropriate books for young readers.

Emerging Readers
(no flags)

Beginning Readers
(1 flag)

Transitional Readers
(2 flags)

Fluent Readers
(3 flags)

These levels are meant only as a guide. All levels are subject to change.

To see a complete list of SandCastle™ books and other nonfiction titles from ABDO Publishing Company, visit **www.abdopublishing.com** or contact us at: 4940 Viking Drive, Edina, Minnesota 55435 • 1-800-800-1312 • fax: 1-952-831-1632